Sababa Cookbook

The Israeli Soul Cookbook

By Rinah Malka
All rights reserved

Published by Rinah Malka

The text and illustrations used in this publication may not reproduced or transmitted in any form by any means, including but not limited to; photocopying, recording, storing in a information retrieval system, without permission of the author, except for the use of brief references to the book for reviewing purposes.

Limited Liability

The information in this book is for educational any entertainment purposes only. Under no circumstances will any legal responsibility or blame be held against the publisher or the author for any damages, reparation, or monetary loss due to information herein.

Copyright © 2019 Rinah Malka

All rights reserved

ISBN: 9781689413398

Sababa Cookbook

Sababa Cookbook

Breakfast 8
Sabich Sandwich 9
Chanukah 'Levivot' (Potato Pancakes) 10
Israeli Breakfast Pizza 11
Shakshuka Avocado 12
Hummus Shakshuka 13
Labneh 14
Walnut Humus Sandwich 15
Kubaneh with Tomato Dip 16
Cold Brew Coffee with Cardamom 17
Green Shakshuka 18

Lunch 20
Israeli Salad 21
Bean Soup (Marak Shuit) 22
Matzah Balls 24
Tabbouleh 25
Kibbeh 26
Salat Avocado (Avocado Salad) 28
Ful Medames (Fava Beans) 29
Matbucha 30
Lentil Soup 31
Yemenite Chicken Soup 32

Dinner 34
Homemade Shawarma 35
Stuffed Eggplant with Lamb 37
Pita Pockets with Chicken and Lentils 39
Stuffed Burekas with Fennel and Potato 41
Lablabi (Chickpea Stew) 42
Lamb Shawarma 44
Whole Wheat Pasta 46
Stuffed Roasted Chicken with Currant and Pine Nuts 47
Israeli Tehina Meatballs 49
Rice with Black Beans and Chickpeas 51

Dips and Snacks 53
Paprika and Chickpeas Hummus 54
Baba Ganoush 55
Beet Dip 56
Spiced Pita Chips 57
Spicy Zhoug 58
Matzo Rolls 59
Sambusaks with Chickpeas 60
Lavash Nachos 61
Tahini Sesame Kale Chips 62
Matbucha 63

Desserts 65
Semolina Cake 66
Charoset 67
Chocolate Swirl Bread 68
Vive Shake 70
Bamba Peanut Butter Mousse 71

Strudel Roll Cookies 72
Halvah-Sesame Sundae 73
Sachlav 75
Cocoa Rose Malabi 76
Walnut Snowball Cookies 77

Sababa Cookbook

BREAKFAST

Sabich Sandwich

Cooking time: 15 mins

Servings: 2

Ingredients:

4 small eggplants, sliced

2 tablespoons oil

2 eggs, hard boiled, sliced

1/4 cup hummus

1/4 cup tahini sauce

2 tablespoons amba sauce

2 pita rounds, cut in half

For the Salad:

1 tomato, diced

1/2 English cucumber, diced

1/4 red onion, diced

1 tablespoon lemon juice

Salt, pepper, to taste

Instructions:

1. Preheat oil in a skillet over medium heat. Add eggplant slices and cook for about 5-7 minutes per side.
2. Mix all salad ingredients in a bowl.
3. Spread hummus on the pita, stuff each pocket with eggplant and eggs.
4. Top with salad and tahini sauce.

Chanukah 'Levivot' (Potato Pancakes)

Cooking time: 15 mins

Servings: 2

Ingredients:

4 potatoes, peeled and grated

2 tablespoons flour

2 egg

1 teaspoon salt

Ground pepper, to taste

Oil

Instructions:

1. Mix potatoes, flour, eggs, salt and pepper in a bowl.
2. Preheat oil in a skillet over medium heat.
3. Spoon the potato mixture onto the skillet and fry pancakes for about 3-4 minutes until browned.
4. Serve.

Israeli Breakfast Pizza

Cooking time:
15 mins

Servings: 6

Ingredients:

1 package pizza dough

1 plum tomato, seeded, grated

3 eggs

2 tablespoons feta cheese

1 tablespoon olive oil

2 tablespoons za'atar spice

Instructions:

1. Preheat the oven to 450°degrees F.
2. Place pizza dough on a flat surface then brush with olive oil. Season with za'atar and sprinkle with cheese. Bake for 6 minutes.
3. Remove from the oven then crack 3 eggs onto the dough. Bake again for 5 minutes, until eggs are properly cooked. Serve with tomato.

Shakshuka Avocado

Cooking time: 20 mins

Servings: 2

Ingredients:

2 avocados

2 eggs

2 basil leaf, chopped

2 teaspoons feta cheese

2 tablespoons marinara sauce

Instructions:

1. Remove the avocado pit and some extra avocado flesh, and then crack an egg into the hole.
2. Using a tin foil, form a bowl around the avocado. Preheat the oven to 425 degrees F.
3. Bake avocado shakshuka for 15 minutes.
4. Top with the sauce, basil and cheese. Serve.

Hummus Shakshuka

Cooking time: 25 mins

Servings: 2

Ingredients:

1 can (14 oz) chopped tomatoes

2 eggs

6 tablespoons humus

1 onion, chopped

1 red pepper, chopped

2 tablespoons cilantro, chopped

1 tablespoon parsley, chopped

1 ½ tablespoons olive oil

1 garlic clove, crushed

1 teaspoon ground cumin

1 teaspoon ground paprika

Instructions:

1. Heat oil in a frying pan over medium heat, cook onions for 3 minutes, stirring occasionally. Add pepper and cook for 5 minutes, stirring often.
2. Add parsley, paprika, garlic, cumin and 1 tablespoon cilantro. Stir and cook for 2 minutes.
3. Stir in tomatoes and cook for 10 minutes. Make two holes in the mixture, crack eggs into them. Cover the pan and cook for 5 minutes.
4. Get two bowls and spread 3 tablespoons humus on the bottom of each one. Scoop half the sauce along with 1 egg (do not break the egg) onto each bowl. Sprinkle with cilantro and serve.

Labneh

Cooking time: 1-2 days

Servings: 8

Ingredients:

1-quart regular yogurt

1 teaspoon salt

Olive oil

Za'atar

Instructions:

1. Mix salt with yogurt in a bowl.
2. Prepare another big bowl and line it with a linen. Pour the mixture on top of the linen and pick up the towel edges, tie at the top.
3. Let hang for about 24-48 hours.
4. Remove the ball that has formed in the bowl. Top with olive oil and za'atar and serve.

Walnut Humus Sandwich

Cooking time:
13 mins

Servings: 2

Ingredients:

½ cup walnuts, toasted, ground

2 cups canned garbanzo beans, drained

1 garlic clove

¼ cup olive oil

4 tablespoons fresh lemon juice

½ cup hot water

1 tablespoon paprika

Pita bread

Instructions:

1. Add 1 ½ cup garbanzo, 2 tablespoons olive oil, 1 garlic clove, lemon juice and walnuts to a food processor and process until smooth.
2. Add a little bit of water from time to time then process until humus is buttery smooth.
3. Add more salt and lemon juice to taste, if necessary.
4. Spread onto pita bread, serve topped with remaining garbanzo, plenty of olive oil, and paprika.

Kubaneh with Tomato Dip

Cooking time: 45 mins

Servings: 3

Ingredients:

1 lb flour

1 tablespoon instant dry yeast + 2 teaspoons

1 ¼ cups (10 oz) butter

1 tablespoon honey

2 tablespoons milk

1 ½ cups warm water

¼ cup brown sugar

2 teaspoons kosher salt

For the Dip:

3 tomatoes, chopped

3 tablespoons cilantro leaves, chopped

1 tablespoon olive oil

1 jalapeno pepper, seeded, chopped

½ teaspoon kosher salt

Instructions:

1. Mix tomato and all the other ingredients for the dip in a bowl. Cover and keep at room temperature.
2. Mix flour, yeast and sugar in a bowl. Add warm water and stir slowly for 2 minutes. Add salt and stir faster for extra 5 minutes. Cover with a towel and keep in a warm place for 1 hour.
3. Heat butter slightly then grease the baking sheets, the working surface, and roller pin with it. Shape the dough into balls. Roll each ball into a paper-thin rectangle then smear with butter, roll into balls again then place next to each other on a baking sheet.
4. Brush the dough with a mixture of honey and milk, then leave for about 40 minutes, covered.
5. Preheat the oven to 400°F and bake for 15 minutes. Reduce the heat to 325°F and bake for extra 30 minutes. When done, let cool for 3 minutes and serve with tomato dip.

Cold Brew Coffee with Cardamom

Cooking time:
15 mins

Servings: 2

Ingredients:

16 oz water

¼ cup ultra-finely ground coffee

8 ground cardamom pods

1/4 teaspoon cinnamon

A pinch of grated ginger

Sugar, to taste

Instructions:

1. Mix coffee, cinnamon, cardamom, ginger, sugar and water in the copper pot, but do not fill to the top.
2. Stir well to combine and preheat the pot over low heat. Do not let it boil, remove from heat just before boiling.
3. Let rest for 20 seconds and heat again until just starts boiling. Let cool and serve.

Green Shakshuka

Cooking time: 30 mins

Servings: 2

Ingredients:

6 cups mixed greens

6 eggs

3 ½ oz goat cheese

1 onion, sliced

3 garlic cloves, chopped

½ fresh jalapeno, seeded, chopped

3 ½ oz sour cream

A pinch of nutmeg

Salt, pepper, to taste

Instructions:

1. Sauté onions for about 9 minutes, then add garlic and cook for 1 minute.
2. Add greens and cook for about 15 minutes, stirring often.
3. Add jalapeno and cook for extra 5 minutes.
4. Stir in sour cream, pepper, salt and nutmeg. Make six holes in the mixture, then crack eggs into them. Stir the egg whites into the mixture and cook for 5 minutes.
5. Serve topped with cheese.

Sababa Cookbook

LUNCH

Israeli Salad

Cooking time: 10 mins

Servings: 4-6

Ingredients:

4 large tomatoes, sliced

4 cucumbers, sliced

2 teaspoons fresh parsley, chopped

1 medium red onion, diced

Feta cheese, cubed

Black olive, diced

3 tablespoons olive oil

½ lemon, juiced

1 teaspoon salt

Instructions:

1. Mix tomatoes, cucumbers, onions, olives, cheese and parsley in a bowl.
2. Top with olive oil, lemon juice and salt, mix together and serve.

Bean Soup (Marak Shuit)

Cooking time:
2 hours 30 mins

Servings: 6

Ingredients:

3 cups canned beans

6 cups chicken broth

1 potato, cubed

1 onion, chopped

3 stalks celery, diced

3 carrots, diced

3 garlic cloves, chopped

3 tablespoons fresh parsley, chopped

2 bay leaves, chopped

6-ounce tomato puree

1 can tomatoes, crushed

1 tablespoon olive oil

1 teaspoon cumin

1 teaspoon thyme, dried

1 paprika

Instructions:

1. Sauté onions in a pan until transparent.
2. Stir in potato, celery, carrot and ½ cup water. Cook for about 5-6 minutes, then transfer to a large pot.
3. Add tomato (both crushed and pureed), beans, garlic, cumin, broth, paprika, parsley, thyme, bay leaves, salt, pepper and sugar, then bring everything to a boil over high heat, stirring often.
4. Reduce the heat to low and cook the soup for extra 1 hour, and serve with pita bread.

1 teaspoon brown sugar

½ teaspoon salt

¼ teaspoon pepper

Pita bread

Matzah Balls

Cooking time: 30 mins

Servings: 12

Ingredients:

4 large eggs

1 cup matzah meal

¼ cup chicken broth

2 tablespoons vegetable oil

Black pepper, freshly ground

Salt

Instructions:

1. Mix eggs, oil, matzah meal, pepper, broth and salt in a bowl. Cover and refrigerate for more than a few hours.
2. Wet your hands in water then shape 12 small balls out of the mixture.
3. Boil water in a large pot then add some salt, add the balls to the pot.
4. Cover and cook for 30 minutes. Serve.

Tabbouleh

Cooking time: 40 mins

Servings: 4-6

Ingredients:

½ cup fine bulgur

½ seedless cucumber, peeled, cored, cut in pieces

2 cups fresh parsley, finely chopped

½ cup fresh mint, finely chopped

2 medium tomatoes, sliced

3 tablespoons fresh lemon juice

3 tablespoons olive oil

1 cup very hot water

¼ teaspoon black pepper

¾ teaspoon salt

Instructions:

1. Mix bulgur and 1 tablespoon oil in heatproof bowl, pour hot water over the mixture, then seal tightly with plastic wrap.
2. Leave for 15 minutes then drain in a sieve. Remove excess liquid.
3. Place bulgur in a bowl then add 2 tablespoons oil, add the remaining ingredients.
4. Stir well and serve.

Kibbeh

Cooking time: 40 mins

Servings: 6-8

Ingredients:

1 lb ground lamb

1 yellow onion, minced

1 1/4 cups fine bulgur wheat, soaked in warm water for 10 minutes, drained

1 teaspoon kosher salt

1 teaspoon ground cumin

1/2 teaspoon ground coriander

For the Filling:

8 oz ground chuck

3 garlic cloves, minced

1 yellow onion, minced

2 teaspoons ground cinnamon

2 teaspoons ground

Instructions:

1. Add lamb, bulgur wheat, salt, cumin, coriander, onion and pepper to a blender and blitz until smooth.
2. Preheat oil in a pan over medium heat. Add onion and garlic and cook for about 5 minutes.
3. Add chuck and all the spices, cook for about 10 minutes. Add pine nuts, stir to combine and remove from the heat.
4. Shape the shell mixture into thin disk and place about 1 tablespoon filling on top and mold the disk around.
5. Preheat oil in a deep pot over medium heat. Add the croquettes and fry for about 5 minutes. Serve.

allspice

2 tablespoons olive oil

1/3 cup pine nuts, toasted

Salt, pepper, to taste

Canola oil, for cooking

Salat Avocado (Avocado Salad)

Cooking time: 10 mins

Servings: 2

Ingredients:

2 avocados, peeled, pitted, diced

1 large tomato, chopped

1 onion, chopped

1 bell pepper, chopped

¼ cup fresh cilantro, chopped

½ fresh lime, juiced

Pepper

Salt

Instructions:

1. Combine avocado, tomato, pepper, cilantro, onion and lime juice in a bowl.
2. Sprinkle with pepper and salt, stir well to combine and serve.

Ful Medames (Fava Beans)

Cooking time:
3 hours

Servings: 6

Ingredients:

2 cups Fava beans, unpeeled, soaked overnight

1/3 cup parsley, chopped

3 lemons, quartered

Olive oil

6 garlic cloves, crushed

Cumin

Chili flakes

Pepper

Salt

Instructions:

1. Drain the beans, add them to the pot and cover with water.
2. Cook for about 2 ½ hours, adding salt when the beans have softened.
3. When the beans are soft, take out two ladles of beans from the pot, including some cooking water. Mash in a bowl and stir back into beans.
4. Top with parsley, olive oil, salt, garlic, chili flakes, cumin and lemons, then serve.

Matbucha

Cooking time: 35 mins

Servings: 6-8

Ingredients:

6 medium ripe tomatoes, cored, chopped

1/3 cup olive oil

1 jalapeno pepper, seeded, diced

½ teaspoon black pepper, freshly ground

6 cloves garlic, peeled, chopped

2 tablespoons paprika

1 ½ teaspoons kosher Salt

Instructions:

1. Cook tomatoes, jalapeno and garlic in a saucepan over medium heat for about 20 minutes, stirring often.
2. Once vegetable are cooked, add oil, black pepper, paprika and salt, and cook for 10 minutes more, stirring often.
3. The dish is ready when the liquid has been absorbed. Serve.

Lentil Soup

**Cooking time:
35 mins**

Servings: 6-8

Ingredients:

1 cup dried lentils, rinsed
2 garlic cloves, minced
2 carrots, shredded
3 cups chicken broth
2 bay leaves
1/8 teaspoon dried thyme
1 cup cooked chicken, diced
1 cup onion, chopped
4 ribs celery, shredded
2 tablespoons fresh parsley, chopped
3 cups water
1/2 teaspoon ground cumin
2 tablespoons lemon juice

Salt, pepper, to taste

Instructions:

1. Add all ingredients except for chicken meat and lemon juice to the pot, stir to combine.
2. Cook covered for about 50-60 minutes.
3. Add lemon juice and chicken meat, cook for 10 minutes more. Serve.

Yemenite Chicken Soup

Cooking time:
3 hours

Servings: 6-8

Ingredients:

1 whole chicken, cut into pieces

4 chicken drumsticks

1 1/4 lbs russet potatoes, peeled and cut into chunks

2 beef marrow bones

1 onion, halved, skin on

2 teaspoons turmeric

3 garlic cloves

1 bunch cilantro, chopped

Salt and pepper, to taste

Instructions:

1. Place chicken and marrow bones into a pan and cover with water. Bring to a boil and cook for about 5 minutes.
2. Add garlic, turmeric, salt and pepper, stir to combine. Add cilantro and onion and bring to a boil again.
3. Reduce the heat to low and cook for about 90 minutes.
4. Remove chicken from the soup and shred. Discard the onion from the soup.
5. Return chicken back to the soup. Add potato and cook for 15-20 minutes more. Serve topped with more cilantro.

Sababa Cookbook

DINNER

Homemade Shawarma

Cooking time:
16 mins

Servings: 4

Ingredients:

1 lb chicken legs, skinless, boneless, sliced into strips

1/3 cup canola oil

1 tablespoon turmeric

1 tablespoon ground coriander

1 teaspoon garlic powder

1 teaspoon cumin

1 teaspoon paprika

1/4 teaspoon cinnamon

1/4 teaspoon ground cloves

½ cup hummus

Cabbage head, chopped

Tomatoes, chopped

4 pitas, warmed

Instructions:

1. Mix oil and all the spices in a bowl. Add chicken and toss well to coat.
2. Cover and refrigerate for at least 1-2 hours.
3. Preheat oil in a skillet over medium heat. Add chicken and cook for about 15 minutes, stirring often.
4. Spread hummus on top of pitas, top with chicken, cabbage and tomato. Serve!

Rinah Malka

Salt, black pepper, to taste	

Stuffed Eggplant with Lamb

Cooking time:
35 mins

Servings: 4

Ingredients:

4 eggplants, halved lengthwise

1 onion, chopped

1 lb ground lamb

1 tablespoon extra-virgin olive oil

3 tablespoons pine nuts

2 teaspoons tomato paste

1/4 cup parsley, chopped

3 teaspoons sugar

1 tablespoon lemon juice

1 teaspoon tamarind concentrate

1 tablespoon ground cinnamon

1 1/2 teaspoons ground cumin

1 1/2 teaspoons sweet

Instructions:

1. Preheat the oven to 425 degrees F. Prepare a baking sheet and line it with parchment paper.
2. Place the eggplants on the baking sheet, brush with oil and season with salt and pepper. Bake for about 20 minutes.
3. Mix cinnamon, cumin and paprika in a bowl. Preheat oil in a skillet over medium heat, add onion and the spices, cook for about 7 minutes.
4. Add lamb and cook for about 5 minutes, stirring often.
5. Add tomato paste, nuts, 1/8 cup parsley, 1 teaspoon sugar, salt and pepper. Stir well to combine everything.
6. Stuff each eggplant with the mixture and place into the baking dish.
7. In a bowl, mix water, lemon juice, tamarind concentrate, remaining sugar, salt and pepper. Pour the mixture into the baking dish.

paprika	8. Add cinnamon stick to the dish, cover with foil and bake for 50 minutes.
1 (1-inch) cinnamon stick	
Salt, pepper, to taste	9. Discard the cinnamon stick and serve eggplants topped with the juices from the dish.

Pita Pockets with Chicken and Lentils

Cooking time: 45 mins

Servings: 4

Ingredients:

8 pitas, warmed

4 cups chicken meat, cooked, shredded

2 tomatoes, chopped

1 head romaine lettuce, shredded

1 cup dried lentils

½ onion, halved

2 ¾ cups water + 6 tablespoons

1 tablespoon olive oil

2 ½ teaspoons salt

1 bay leaf

½ cup bulgur

1 ½ teaspoons hot sauce

½ cup tahini

Instructions:

1. Preheat the oven to 350 degrees F.
2. Mix lentils, water, onion, oil, salt and bay leaf in a saucepan and bring everything to a boil. Cook for 15 minutes.
3. Add bulgur and cook for about 12 minutes more, stirring from time to time.
4. Remove from heat and add hot sauce. Let rest covered for 5 minutes. Remove the bay leaf and onion.
5. Mix tahini, 6 tablespoons water, garlic, lemon juice, salt and yogurt in a bowl.
6. Cut the top third off of each pita. Stuff each pocket with lentil mixture, add chicken, tomatoes and the sauce. Top with lettuce and serve.

Rinah Malka

2 garlic cloves, minced 5 teaspoons lemon juice 1 cup plain yogurt	

Stuffed Burekas with Fennel and Potato

Cooking time: 45 mins

Servings: 5

Ingredients:

5 Yukon Gold potatoes, diced

1 fennel bulb, chopped

1 shallot, chopped

2 cups celery, sliced

½ cup extra virgin olive oil

1 cup feta cheese

1/2 teaspoon cinnamon

1/2 teaspoon cardamom

2 tablespoons za-atar

1 tablespoon anise seed

1 package phyllo dough

Salt, pepper, to taste

Instructions:

1. Preheat oil in a pan over medium heat. Add celery, fennel and shallot and cook for about 3-4 minutes.
2. Add potatoes, cheese, cinnamon, cardamom, za'atar, anise seeds, salt and pepper, stir well to combine. Cook for about 1-2 minutes. Remove from heat.
3. Preheat the oven to 350 degrees F. Prepare a cooking sheet and coat it with cooking spray.
4. Place the dough onto the baking sheet, cut into sheets. Top with the filling mixture. Fold into rolls and brush with oil. Cook for 25 minutes.

Lablabi (Chickpea Stew)

Cooking time:
2 hours

Servings: 10

Ingredients:

2 lbs chickpeas, soaked in water overnight, rinsed and drained

12 cups water

2 onions, peeled

12 peppercorns, in a teaball

2 bay leaves, cracked

1 tablespoon cumin seeds, toasted

1 teaspoon coriander seeds, toasted

1 dry hot chile, toasted

5 garlic cloves, minced

8 scallions, sliced

4 tablespoons olive oil

3 lemons, juiced

Instructions:

1. Mix chickpeas, water, onions, peppercorns and bay leaves in a saucepan. Add salt and bring to a boil. Cook over low heat for 1-2 hours.

2. Ground cumin seeds and coriander seeds in a mortar. Add garlic, spice mix and salt, pound until ground. Add shallot and pound too.

3. Preheat oil in a skillet over medium heat. Add chile and garlic paste and cook for about 1 minute.

4. Add the mixture to the chickpeas and simmer for 10-20 minutes more. Add lemon juice and cook for 1-2 minutes.

5. Serve topped with lemon wedges and baguette slices.

Sababa Cookbook

Salt, to taste

Lemon wedges, for serving

Baguettes, for serving

Lamb Shawarma

Cooking time: 30 mins

Servings: 4

Ingredients:

3 lbs lamb leg, sliced

1 bell pepper

5 garlic cloves, sliced

2 carrots, sliced

1 teaspoon sumac

2 teaspoons cumin

1/2 teaspoon cinnamon

1/2 teaspoon cayenne pepper

2 tablespoons brown sugar

1/2 cup water + 1 tablespoon

1/2 cup rice wine vinegar

1 tablespoon sugar

1 serrano chili pepper

1/2 cup parsley

1/2 cup cilantro

4 tablespoons vegetable oil

Instructions:

1. Mix sumac, cumin, salt, pepper, sugar and cinnamon in a bowl. Season lamb neat with the seasoning mix and drizzle with oil. Toss to coat and refrigerate overnight.
2. Mix carrots, salt, vinegar and sugar in a bowl. Toss to coat and refrigerate overnight.
3. Mix serrano, parsley, cilantro, garlic, oil, water, cumin, pepper flakes and salt in blender and blitz until smooth. This will be the green sauce.
4. Preheat oil in a skillet and add lamb meat, cook until brown on all sides.
5. Heat the pitas in an oven for several mixture. Stuff each pita bread with lamb, sauce, vegetables and carrots. Serve with more green sauce.

Sababa Cookbook

1 teaspoon lemon juice

1/4 teaspoon cumin

1/2 teaspoon red pepper flakes

Salt, pepper, to taste

Lettuce, chopped

1 tomato, chopped

1/2 cucumber, chopped

Pita breads, warmed

Whole Wheat Pasta

Cooking time: 20 mins

Servings: 4-6

Ingredients:

1 bag whole wheat pasta

1 small container red cherry tomatoes

1 small container yellow cherry tomatoes

2 garlic cloves

1 onion

1 bag baby spinach

1 packet fresh basil

Black pepper, diced

2 lemons, juiced

4 cups frozen humus beans

Olive oil

1 cup water

Kosher salt

Instructions:

1. Cook pasta according to package instructions.
2. Sauté onions, pepper and salt in ½ tablespoon olive oil. Add spinach and cook until wilted. Add beans, juice of 1 lemon and water, then cook for 7 minutes. Add extra pepper and salt to taste.
3. Pour pasta into sauce and mix together. Add basil leaves, cherry tomatoes and remaining olive oil, plus juice of lemon. Serve.

Stuffed Roasted Chicken with Currant and Pine Nuts

**Cooking time:
90 mins**

Servings: 8

Ingredients:

1 whole chicken

4 carrots, sliced

2 onions, diced

2 turnips, diced

2 cups chicken broth

1 lb ground chicken

1 tablespoon olive oil

1/4 teaspoon allspice

1/4 teaspoon coriander

1/4 teaspoon cinnamon

2 garlic cloves, chopped

1 ½ cup rice, cooked

3 tablespoon pine nuts

Instructions:

1. Toast pine nuts in a skillet over medium heat, for 3-4 minutes. Transfer to a plate.
2. Add oil to the skillet and add ground chicken, allspice, coriander, cinnamon, garlic, salt and pepper, cook for about 5-6 minutes.
3. Add rice, nuts, currants and mint, stir well to combine. Let cool completely.
4. Stuff the chicken with the cooked mixture, rub with salt and pepper.
5. Preheat the oven to 350 degrees F. Place the chicken into the baking dish and bake for 30 minutes.
6. Add all the vegetables to the dish and roast for 60 minutes more.
7. Let rest for 10 minutes before serving.

Rinah Malka

2 tablespoon currants

1 tablespoon fresh mint, chopped

Salt, pepper, to taste

Israeli Tehina Meatballs

Cooking time: 45 mins

Servings: 8

Ingredients:

16 oz Tehina + 5 tablespoons water

2 lbs lean ground meat

1 onion, minced

3 garlic cloves, minced

1/2 cup breadcrumbs

2 eggs, beaten

3/4 cup parsley, chopped

1/2 teaspoon cinnamon

1 teaspoon cumin

1 teaspoon turmeric

1/4 teaspoon ginger powder

1 teaspoon paprika

2 tablespoons pine nuts, roasted

Instructions:

1. Mix tehina and water in a pot. Stir well to combine.
2. Mix meat, onion, garlic, breadcrumbs, eggs, parsley, cinnamon, cumin, turmeric, ginger powder, paprika, pine nuts, salt and pepper in a bowl. Mix well to combine.
3. Shape the mixture into balls.
4. Preheat oil in a skillet over medium heat. Add meatballs and cook for about 2-3 minutes per side.
5. Transfer to a baking dish. Preheat the oven to 350 degrees F. Add Tehina mixture to the dish and bake for 30 minutes.
6. Serve topped with parsley.

2 tablespoons canola oil

Salt, pepper, to taste

Rice with Black Beans and Chickpeas

Cooking time:
45 mins

Servings: 8

Ingredients:

1 ½ lbs ground turkey

2 cans (15 oz each) chickpeas, rinsed and drained

2 cans (15 oz each) black beans, rinsed and drained

1 cup rice, uncooked

1 garlic clove, minced

1 tablespoon olive oil

2 teaspoons cumin

2 teaspoons coriander

1 teaspoon turmeric

1 teaspoon cayenne pepper

4 cups chicken stock

Salt, pepper, to taste

Instructions:

1. Preheat oil in a skillet over medium heat. Add meat and cook until brown. Transfer to a plate.
2. Add garlic to the same pan and cook for about 1 minute. Add rice, cumin, coriander, turmeric, and cayenne. Cook for about 5 minutes.
3. Add chicken stock and bring everything to a boil.
4. Reduce the heat to low and cook for 20 minutes.
5. Mix rice, meat, chickpeas and beans and stir to combine. Season with salt and pepper and serve.

Rinah Malka

Dips and Snacks

Paprika and Chickpeas Hummus

**Cooking time:
45 mins**

Servings: 8

Ingredients:

1/2 lb dried chickpeas

1 tablespoon baking soda

7 garlic cloves, unpeeled

1/2 cup extra-virgin olive oil

1/4 teaspoon ground cumin

1/2 cup tahini, at room temperature

1/4 cup lemon juice

1/4 cup parsley, chopped

Salt, pepper, to taste

Instructions:

1. Cover chickpeas with water and add baking soda. Refrigerate overnight. Drain and rinse.
2. Add rinsed and drained chickpeas to the pot and cover with water. Add garlic and bring everything to a boil.
3. Cook over low heat for about 40 minutes. Drain and reserve about ½ cup cooking water. Rinse the chickpeas and peel the garlic cloves.
4. Add chickpeas, cooking water, oil and garlic to a blender and process until smooth.
5. Add tahini, lemon juice and cumin, blitz until smooth again. Season with salt and pepper.
6. Serve sprinkled with cumin and paprika.

Baba Ganoush

Cooking time: 45 mins

Servings: 4

Ingredients:

5 eggplants, trimmed

2 tablespoons lemon juice

½ lemon, zested

2 tablespoons extra virgin olive oil

1 tablespoon tahini

1 garlic clove, minced

1 tablespoon parsley, chopped

5 basil leaves, chopped

1 tablespoon pine nuts, toasted

Salt, pepper, to taste

Instructions:

1. Preheat the broiler and broil the eggplants for about 45 minutes, flipping once halfway. Let cool completely.
2. Scoop out the inside of each eggplant and drain.
3. Mix eggplant flesh with oil, lemon juice and zest, tahini, garlic, salt and pepper in a bowl.
4. Serve topped with pine nuts.

Beet Dip

Cooking time: 1 hour

Servings: 4

Ingredients:

6 beets, trimmed

2 scallions, sliced

2 garlic cloves, minced

1 red chile, seeded and minced

2 tablespoons goat cheese, crumbled

1/4 cup hazelnuts, toasted, chopped

1 cup plain Greek yogurt

3 tablespoons extra-virgin olive oil

1 1/2 tablespoons maple syrup

1 tablespoon za'atar

Salt, pepper, to taste

Instructions:

1. Preheat the oven to 350 degrees F.
2. Add beets to the baking dish and pour about ¼ cup water inside. Cover with foil and bake for 1 hour. Let cool.
3. Peel the beets and chop, add to a blender. Add the remaining ingredients and blitz until smooth. Serve.

Spiced Pita Chips

Cooking time:
25 minutes

Servings: 8

Ingredients:

1 package pocket pitas, split horizontally and cut into wedges

1/4 cup olive oil

1 tablespoon za'atar

1 teaspoon sweet paprika

Salt, to taste

Instructions:

1. Preheat the oven to 350 degrees F.
2. Brush pitas with oil, season with salt, paprika and za'atar.
3. Spread the pita wedges onto the baking sheet and bake for 20 minutes until golden.
4. Let cool before serving.

Spicy Zhoug

Cooking time: 20 mins

Servings: 4

Ingredients:

2 Hungarian wax peppers, seeded and chopped

2 garlic cloves

1 cup cilantro, chopped

1/2 cup parsley leaves

1/2 teaspoon ground coriander

1/2 teaspoon ground cumin

1/4 cup extra-virgin olive oil

1 1/2 teaspoons red wine vinegar

1/4 cup pumpkin seeds, toasted, shelled

Salt, pepper, to taste

Instructions:

1. Add all ingredients to a blender or a food processor. Blitz until coarsely chopped and combined.
2. Cover and refrigerate before serving.

Matzo Rolls

Cooking time: 40 mins

Servings: 4

Ingredients:

2 cups matzo cake meal

¼ cup margarine

2 cups water

¼ cup vegetable oil

6 eggs

Salt, to taste

Instructions:

1. Add water to a pan and bring to a boil.
2. Add oil, margarine and salt, stir well to combine and return to a boil.
3. Add matzo cake meal and stir well until you get lumpy dough.
4. Let cool slightly and add eggs, combine until the mixture is smooth. Let rest for about 30 minutes.
5. Preheat the oven to 350 degrees F. Shape the mixture into balls and place onto the baking sheet. Bake for 30 minutes.
6. Let rest for about 10 minutes before serving.

Sambusaks with Chickpeas

Cooking time:
1 hour 10 mins

Servings: 4

Ingredients:

1 ½ cups flour

1 tablespoon cornstarch

1 teaspoon baking powder

1 onion, chopped

11 eggs

1 can (15 oz) garbanzo beans, drained and lightly mashed

¼ bunch cilantro, chopped

1/3 cup warm water

1 teaspoon ground cumin

1 teaspoon ground coriander

Salt, pepper, to taste

Vegetable oil

Instructions:

1. Mix flour, cornstarch, salt, baking powder, 3 tablespoons vegetable oil and water in a bowl. Cover and let rest for 10 minutes.
2. Shape the dough into balls and roll each ball in more flour, roll out into circles.
3. Preheat oil in a skillet and add onion, cook for about 5-6 minutes.
4. Add beans, cilantro, cumin, coriander, salt, and pepper, stir well to combine.
5. Slightly cook eggs in a microwave (for about 40 seconds).
6. Preheat about 2 cups oil in a deep pan over medium heat. Spoon the bean on top of each dough circle, add cooked egg and fold into half-moon shape, seal.
7. Fry in hot oil for about 3 minutes per side. Remove to a plate covered with paper towel, serve.

Lavash Nachos

Cooking time: 10 mins

Servings: 4

Ingredients:

4 sheets lavash, cut into triangles

1 can cannellini beans, drained and rinsed

1 white onion, chopped

4 oz mozzarella, shredded

16 oz guacamole, for serving

Instructions:

1. Preheat the oven to 350 degrees F. Prepare a cookie sheet and line it with parchment paper.
2. Spread the lavash triangles on the baking sheet and bake for about 5 minutes.
3. Transfer the baked chips to a baking pan and top with beans, onions and cheese, bake for about 5 minutes.
4. Serve topped with guacamole, if desired.

Tahini Sesame Kale Chips

Cooking time:
2 hours

Servings: 8

Ingredients:

1 bunch kale, washed and dried

2 limes, juiced

2 tablespoons olive oil

¼ cup tahini

1 tablespoon sesame seeds

1 teaspoon red pepper flakes

Salt, pepper, to taste

Instructions:

1. Preheat the oven to 175 degrees F. Prepare a cookie sheet and line it with parchment paper.
2. Remove kale leaves from stems, cut into medium sized pieces. Spread onto the baking sheet in one layer.
3. Mix lime juice, oil, tahini, sesame seeds, pepper flakes, salt and pepper in a bowl. Pour the mixture onto the kale leaves and toss to combine.
4. Bake for about 2 hours, flipping once halfway. Let cool before serving.

Matbucha

Cooking time: 20 mins

Servings: 4

Ingredients:

2 bell peppers

1 lb tomatoes

2 tablespoons olive oil

2 jalapenos or any other long spicy peppers

2 garlic cloves, chopped

1 tablespoons white wine

1/2 teaspoon ground coriander

1/2 teaspoon ground cumin

1/2 teaspoon paprika

1/2 lemon, juiced

1/2 cup cilantro, chopped

Instructions:

1. Preheat a grill to medium high heat. Put the peppers on the grill directly on the gas burner and cook until charred on all sides. Let cool, peel and core.
2. Bring a pot of water to a boil and add tomatoes. Remove from hot water and rinse with cold water. Peel the skin.
3. Preheat oil in a pan over medium heat. Chop peppers and tomatoes and add to the pan.
4. Add the remaining ingredients, except for cilantro, stir to combine, cook for about 20 minutes, stirring from time to time. Serve topped with cilantro.

Rinah Malka

DESSERTS

Semolina Cake

Cooking time: 35 mins

Servings: 12

Ingredients:

3 cups semolina flour

1 cup sugar + 2 cups

2 teaspoons tahini

1 cup shredded coconut, unsweetened

¼ cup butter

2 cups plain yogurt

¼ teaspoon baking soda

4 teaspoons baking powder

2 ½ cups water

Instructions:

1. Preheat the oven to 400 degrees F. Prepare a baking pan and coat with cooking spray.
2. Spread about 1 teaspoon tahini over the bottom of the pan.
3. Mix flour, 1 cups sugar, butter and coconut in a bowl.
4. In a separate bowl, mix yogurt, baking powder and baking soda.
5. Combine two mixtures together, stir until incorporated. Pour the batter into the pan and bake for about 30-35 minutes.
6. Mix water and 2 cups sugar in a pot over medium heat. Cook until sugar dissolves, stirring all the time. Let cool slightly and pour over ready cake. Serve.

Charoset

Cooking time: 15 mins

Servings: 10

Ingredients:

2 apples, quartered, cored

3 bananas, chopped

1 cup walnuts, chopped

1 cup dates, pitted

2 tablespoons matzo meal

1 orange, zested and juiced

1 lemon, zested and juiced

2 teaspoons cinnamon

2 teaspoons sugar

1/3 cup red wine

Instructions:

1. Add sugar, apples, bananas, walnuts, dates, orange zest and juice, lemon zest and juice and cinnamon to a blender or a food processor and blitz until coarsely chopped.
2. Transfer to a bowl and add wine, stir to combine.
3. Add matzo meal and stir well to combine. Cover and refrigerate before serving.

Chocolate Swirl Bread

Cooking time: 20 mins

Servings: 8

Ingredients:

3 ¾ cups bread flour

2 ¼ teaspoons dry active yeast

1/4 cup brown sugar + 1 teaspoon

1 ¼ cups warm soymilk

1/4 cup unsalted margarine, cubed

1/2 teaspoon nutmeg

1 teaspoon cardamom

3/4 teaspoon kosher salt

1 egg, at room temperature

1 tablespoon baking powder

1/4 cup water

For the Filling:

Instructions:

1. Preheat the oven to 275 degrees F. Prepare a baking sheet and spread the baking powder onto it. Bake for 30 minutes. Transfer to an air tight container and seal.

2. Mix yeast, 1 teaspoon brown sugar and ¼ cup milk in a bowl. Let rest for about 5 minutes, the mixture should begin to rise.

3. Mix margarine with the remaining milk in a separate bowl, beat well. Add egg, salt and spices. Add the yeast mixture and stir to combine. Slowly add flour and mix until smooth. The batter should not be very sticky, add more flour if needed.

4. Grease a large bowl with oil and add dough, cover and let rest for 2 hours until risen.

5. Transfer the dough onto the floured surface and roll out in a rectangle. Spread the chocolate spread onto the dough, sprinkle with chocolate chips on top. Wrap the dough into a roll and place into the loaf pan. Cover

2/3 cup chocolate spread 1/4 cup chocolate chips	and let rest for 30 minutes. 6. Mix baking powder and ¼ cup water in a bowl. Brush the cake with the mixture. 7. Preheat the oven to 375 degrees F. Bake the cake for 20 minutes. Cover the pan with foil and cook for 20 minutes more. Serve.

Vive Shake

Cooking time: 5 mins

Servings: 2

Ingredients:

12 oz vanilla yogurt

2 peaches, frozen, sliced

¾ cup orange juice

½ cup slivered almonds

½ cup granola

Instructions:

1. Add all ingredients to a blender or a food processor and blitz until smooth.
2. Pour into chilled glasses and serve.

Bamba Peanut Butter Mousse

Cooking time:
20 mins

Servings: 10

Ingredients:

5 oz roasted peanuts, crushed

1/3 cup all-purpose flour

1/2 teaspoon black pepper

1/2 cup brown sugar

1/2 cup unsalted margarine, softened

1 ½ cups smooth peanut butter

3 cups whipping cream

1/2 cup confectioner sugar

1 teaspoon ginger

1 ½ tablespoons vanilla extract

1/2 teaspoon salt

Instructions:

1. Mix peanuts, flour, pepper and brown sugar in a bowl. Add margarine and mix with your hands until crumbly.
2. Preheat the oven to 350 degrees F. Prepare a baking sheet and line it with parchment paper.
3. Pour the peanuts mixture onto the baking sheet and spread evenly. Bake for about 15 minutes. Let cool.
4. Mix peanut butter and whipping cream in a heat proof bowl and microwave for 30 seconds. Stir well until smooth.
5. Add ginger, salt and vanilla and beat until combined. Add confectioners' sugar, stir well.
6. Divide the baked peanut brittle among cups and top with the mouse. Cover and refrigerate before serving.

Strudel Roll Cookies

Cooking time: 20 mins

Servings: 12-16

Ingredients:

3 cups flour

7 tablespoons butter

5 tablespoons jam of choice

1 cup sour cream

½ cup raisins

1 cup coconut flakes

¾ cup walnuts, chopped

1 cup sesame seeds

A pinch of salt

Instructions:

1. Mix flour, butter, sour cream and salt in a bowl. Stir well until smooth and refrigerate for 1 hour.
2. Preheat the oven to 350 degrees F.
3. Mix raisins, coconut, nuts and sesame seeds in a separate bowl.
4. Roll out the dough on a floured surface. Spread jam and raisins mixture on top and wrap into a roll. Cut into cookies and place them on a baking sheet lined with parchment paper.
5. Bake for 15-20 minutes. Let cool slightly before serving.

Halvah-Sesame Sundae

Cooking time: **45 mins**

Servings: 8

Ingredients:

8 egg yolks

3/4 cup sugar + ½ cup

3 cups whole milk

1 ½ cups heavy cream

2 teaspoons toasted sesame oil

2 teaspoons pure vanilla extract

1/4 teaspoon salt

1 1/2 tablespoons honey

1/3 cup tahini

1/2 cup halvah, crumbled

Instructions:

1. Mix milk, 1 cup cream, ½ cup sugar in a saucepan and bring to a boil. Stir until sugar dissolves.
2. Beat egg yolks and ¼ cup sugar in a bowl. Slowly add milk mixture to the egg mixture and place over low heat. Cook for about 4 minutes, stirring often.
3. Add sesame oil, vanilla and salt, stir well and let cool.
4. Pour the mixture to the ice cream making machine and process as per the instructions. Transfer to a container and freeze for 2 hours.
5. Add ½ cup sugar to a saucepan and place over low heat. Cook for about 2 minutes.
6. Remove from heat and add about ½ cup water, return to the heat. Cook until sugar dissolves, for about 3 minutes, stirring all the time. Transfer to a bowl.
7. Add ½ cup cream and honey to the saucepan and bring to a boil. Remove from heat and add tahini, stir to combine.

	8. Serve ice cream with caramel mixture and tahini mixture on top. Sprinkle with halvah.

Sachlav

Cooking time: 5 mins

Servings: 2

Ingredients:

3 cups coconut milk

1 tablespoon sugar

2 teaspoons vanilla extract

2 tablespoons cornstarch

½ teaspoon rose water

A pinch sea salt

Instructions:

1. Add milk, sugar, vanilla, cornstarch, rose water and salt in a pan. Place over low heat and bring to a boil.
2. Cook for about 3 minutes, stirring constantly. Pour into cups and serve.

Cocoa Rose Malabi

Cooking time: 10 mins

Servings: 6

Ingredients:

4 cups almond milk

¼ cup cocoa powder

1/3 cup honey

½ cup cornstarch

1 tablespoon rose water

Instructions:

1. Mix about 3 ½ cups milk, honey and cocoa powder in a pan and place over low heat. Heat for about 3 minutes, stirring all the time.
2. Mix cornstarch and remaining milk in a bowl. Add to the warm milk mixture, stir to combine.
3. Cook for about 4-5 minutes, stirring often. Remove from heat.
4. Add rose water and let cool. Refrigerate before serving.

Walnut Snowball Cookies

Cooking time: 30 mins

Servings: 8

Ingredients:

2 cups flour

1 ½ cups walnuts

2 sticks unsalted butter, at room temperature

2 teaspoons vanilla extract

2 cups confectioners' sugar

1/4 teaspoon salt

Instructions:

1. Preheat the oven to 350 degrees F. Prepare a cookie sheet and line it with parchment paper.
2. Spread the nuts onto the baking sheet and toast for about 8-10 minutes. Let cool and chop.
3. Beat butter and vanilla in a bowl. Add 1 cup sugar and beat until fluffy.
4. Add salt, flour and walnuts, beat until smooth and combined.
5. Reduce the oven temperature to 325 degrees F.
6. Shape the mixture into small balls. Place on the baking sheet and bake for 15-17 minutes. Let cool slightly.
7. Roll each ball in the remaining sugar and serve.

Made in the USA
Middletown, DE
22 July 2022